GW01402901

Original title:
The Comfort of Knitted Days

Author: Nora Sinclair
ISBN HARDBACK: 978-9916-94-368-7
ISBN PAPERBACK: 978-9916-94-369-4

Nestled in Fiber

In a world where stitches play,
I dive into yarn, hip-hip-hooray!
My needles click with cheerful chat,
While cats plot mischief with a spat.

Woolly warriors dance with glee,
As I trip on that rogue ball, tee-hee!
My friends all say, 'You knit so neat!'
But they don't see my tangled feet!

A Symphony of Texture and Time

A melody of clinking is my tune,
As I knit beneath a bright, full moon.
Yarn balls tumble and round they go,
Oh, what a show, oh, what a show!

Each loop and purl a catchy beat,
My cat, the conductor, takes a seat.
Some socks are left with holes so grand,
Yet in my heart, they proudly stand!

Radiance in Hues of Yarn

Colors pop and twirl in my hand,
I've yarn like a rainbow, oh so grand!
While I jest and twist like a playful breeze,
The sweater I craft pulls me to my knees!

With shades of laughter, I make my stash,
Every misstep becomes a splash.
In hues so bright, I strut with pride,
But dear sweater, could you please abide?

The Craft of Slow Living

In cozy corners where time does bend,
I slowly craft my new soft friend.
Each stitch a giggle, each row a cheer,
A scarf to warm me throughout the year!

Yet somehow I'm left with snakes of yarn,
And Pinterest dreams that make me yarn!
With every loop, I nod and grin,
Who knew crafting could feel like a win?

The Arc of Warm Threads

In cozy corners we conspire,
With yarn and needles, never tire.
We laugh at knots that give us strife,
Creating chaos, oh what a life!

With every stitch, a giggle bursts,
A tangled tale that never thirsts.
Our masterpieces—clumsy and bright,
Fashioned in daylight, a comical sight!

Oh, how the colors twist and twirl,
Our frantic fingers start to swirl.
A beanie here, a scarf over there,
Each slip of yarn, a whimsical dare!

When someone asks, "What's that supposed to be?"
We shrug, "It's art, can't you see?"
In the laughter, we find delight,
In our imperfect creations, pure insight!

Hearts Woven Together

In a flurry of fibers, we find our glee,
Casting on memories, just you and me.
With each crazy purl, we share a laugh,
As the yarn decides it wants to take a bath!

Oh, the patterns break, and stitches stray,
We marvel at chaos in a colorful way.
Like spaghetti tangled in a fun fight,
Our knitting adventures bring pure delight!

With needles clicking, like a tap dance,
Our antics abound, a silly romance.
We create mismatched gifts, wrapped with a grin,
It's the joy of togetherness that makes us win!

So here's to our knots, our rickety lines,
In this crafty mess, our friendship shines.
With laughter and yarn, we knit with flair,
Hearts woven together, a wonderful pair!

Warmth Beneath the Needles

Fingers dance with wooly cheer,
Casting doubts into the rear.
A tangled mess is pure delight,
My cat thinks it's a playtime fight.

With a twist and purl, we joke around,
Our laughter echoes, warms the ground.
Each stitch a giggle, a quirky tale,
My coffee's gone cold, but who could fail?

A Tapestry of Calm

Yarn balls tumble, they have a plan,
To weave a chaos, oh yes, they can!
A daring knot, a cunning twist,
Oops! That was not on my to-do list.

Stitch by stitch, we'll mend the fray,
With glittering eyes, we shout hooray!
Laughter fills the air, it's bliss,
As I make a scarf, my hat's amiss.

Soft Stitches in Quiet Hours

In cozy corners, we sit tight,
With threads of humor, hearts take flight.
A knitting mishap turns to cheer,
My scarf now doubles as a beer.

The clock ticks slow, but laughter's fast,
As yarn joins us for a splendid cast.
We sip our tea, and then we muse,
Who needs a pattern? We'll just choose!

The Rhythm of Tension and Release

Needles clink with rhythmic grace,
Chatting merrily in our space.
A rogue stitch here, a playful yawn,
That sweater looks more like a prawn.

Each row a giggle, each turn a tease,
As tea spills over, oh, what a breeze!
We weave our tales with every loop,
Sometimes the yarn, it's just a goof.

Threads of Tranquility

In a world tangled like my yarn,
I sip my tea, avoiding the barn.
My cat jumps high, just for a laugh,
Chasing at shadows, taking my half.

The needles click with a playful song,
As I knit a sweater, oh so wrong!
A pattern lost, but who can tell?
It's cozy chaos — and all is well.

Tapestry of Quiet Moments

Around the fire, we sit and weave,
Stories unravel, it's hard to believe.
A blanket of laughter, row upon row,
It keeps us warm when the teasing winds blow.

Knots in the yarn, just like our hearts,
Sometimes they tangle, but that's where it starts.
With each purl and knit, we chase the stress,
A tapestry formed in pure silliness.

Yarn Between Heartbeats

Stitch by stitch, we dance in delight,
Yarn flings about, oh what a sight!
Jokes tossed like balls of bright, soft thread,
We giggle and snicker, no worries ahead.

A scarf that could reach from here to the moon,
I'm crafting a treasure, while humming a tune.
Mistakes? Who cares? We just laugh and play,
This yarn dance is wild, come join the fray!

The Weave of Whispered Dreams

In a land where stitches come alive,
Pants made from yarn, can you believe?
I trip on my project, it's quite absurd,
But laughter's the thread that we've all heard.

With each little loop, a giggle erupts,
Catching my dog as he joyfully jumps.
We weave our dreams with each silly thread,
In this playful mess, no need for the bed.

Fibers of Forgotten Lullabies

Yarns once tangled in time's embrace,
A cat naps softly in my favorite space.
Needles clicking like a metronome's song,
Each stitch whispers where the lost belong.

In a world of loops, I find my delight,
While tangled threads play hide and seek at night.
A bobbin's dance, a playful twirl,
Turning chaos into a cozy swirl.

Cozy Afternoons in Stitches

Each afternoon begins with a cup,
A drop of tea serves cheer to sup.
Laughter pops like bubbles in the air,
While colorful fibers become my flair.

With a twist and turn, I craft my design,
A scarf or a hat, oh, how they'll shine!
My friend's wild tales wind through each row,
As our laughter dances, soft as the snow.

Knit One, Breathe Two

Knit one, breathe two, it's a fun little game,
Got lost in the yarn, now I've lost track of the name.
Misplaced a stitch, but who needs to care?
I'm creating a creature with two mismatched eyes to
spare!

Crochet hooks fly like bees in the sun,
Who knew this craft would be so much fun?
A yarn cake plops and rolls in delight,
And socks in the making bring giggles at night.

Warmth Woven in Whimsy

A blanket of colors spills 'cross the floor,
My feet get lost, but my heart wants more.
Laughter echoes with each playful twist,
Oh, the joy of a yarn stash that can't be missed!

With a purl and a yarn, we weave silly dreams,
Knitting together life's whimsical themes.
Orange and purple, they dance on the hook,
Creating a story, a joyful nook.

Calm in Every Twist

In a world of yarn and cheer,
I knit away my daily fear.
With needles clicking, oh so fast,
I laugh at how this day has passed.

A tangled mess, a purl or two,
I swear this yarn has got a clue.
A hat for the cat, or socks for me,
What's next? A sweater for a tree?

Rows of stitches, I make my way,
Mismatched patterns brighten my day.
With each one's loop, a giggle grows,
Who knew a hobby could propose?

In colorful threads my worries pause,
I twirl and whirl without a cause.
Knitting brings a jolly light,
As I dance with yarn till night.

Handcrafted Hues of Home

Wooly wonders fill my space,
Crafting joy at a goofy pace.
I knit a blanket for the chair,
But find it's now a llama's hair.

Teaspoon's missing, oh my dear,
I used it to unknit my fear.
Each stitch a giggle, looped with glee,
I think my cat has learned to see!

Stripes and polka dots collide,
A fashion statement, I won't hide.
In bright pink knickers, what a sight,
I prance around, oh what a fright!

Friends gather 'round my little nest,
They chuckle, "This is quite the jest!"
Yet in each fiber, there's no fuss,
Just laughter, love, and joyful trust.

Woven Dreams Beneath the Sun

Under warm sun, I take my seat,
With yarn and laughs, the day's a treat.
Rows of stitches, sun upon my face,
A garden of colors, a happy place.

I tie a knot, watch the breeze,
As stitches dance like happy bees.
With one big twist, I'm caught off guard,
My yarn's become a jumpy bard!

Knitting socks that fit my cat,
I give a laugh, and then I chat.
"Dear kitty, you're now quite chic,
With needle in hand, I'm feeling sleek!"

Clouds appear, but never mind,
With every loop, pure bliss I find.
Under this sky, I'll intertwine,
With each big stitch, the day is fine.

Patterns of Contentment

From skeins of joy, I craft a tale,
With each new stitch, I gladly sail.
Two purls, a knit, then a twisty fate,
Creating art that giggles great.

The couch is lined with chaos bright,
With yarnballs rolling in pure delight.
As patterns blend and mishaps roam,
I smile wide, for this is home.

Peering at what I've made today,
A cozy monster, or so they say.
With quirky shapes and colors grand,
My handiwork takes to the land.

With laughter echoing through the hall,
Each crafted piece tells tales of all.
In every thread a story spins,
In happy stitches, the fun begins.

The Gentle Pull of Yarn

In a world where stitches fly,
My yarn ball starts to sigh.
It tumbles down the hall with glee,
A merry chase for you and me.

The cat surveys with narrowed eyes,
The art of pouncing, such a prize!
I love it when she takes a leap,
My tangled mess, her lofty heap.

With needles clack and laughter loud,
A knitting circle, snug and proud.
We gossip 'bout the latest trends,
While plotting who will knit amends.

In vibrant hues of teal and red,
Mistakes are made, but never dread.
We take a snip, we take a twist,
How funny is the yarn we've missed!

Stitches that Bind

With needles clicking, what a sound,
A better place can't be found.
A cozy nook, we share our tales,
As yarn begins to dance like whales.

My project's growing, oh so slow,
It looks like something from a show!
A sweater? Scarf? Who really cares?
It's mostly yarn, like tangled hairs.

I dropped a stitch, oh dear, oh my!
A yarn explosion, it flew high!
We laugh and roll upon the floor,
Knots like puzzles we can't ignore.

With every loop, a little cheer,
This crafty joy, we hold so dear.
And if it's bad, we'll call it art,
The beauty lies in every part!

The Fabric of Familiar Days

In sunlit rooms, we toss our strings,
Like silly cats, we dabble in flings.
Each fiber holds a memory bright,
A cozy hug that feels just right.

Patterns promised to behave,
But life is strange, like knitting a wave.
Frogging stitches feels so fun,
We laugh while teasing everyone!

A tangled mess, a comical plight,
'What is this thing?' we'd ask in fright.
Yet through the chaos and the yarn,
We find the charm and fray's sweet dawn.

Through patterns strange and colors wild,
Crafting joy, we're forever styled.
In our crazy quilt, we'll always find,
A patchwork love that's truly blind!

Woolen Whispers at Dusk

As evening creeps, we share our craft,
With wools and threads, we all just laughed.
Each project hides a tale to tell,
Of stitches that slipped and yarn that fell.

Our needles click, a heartwarming tune,
The moon peeks in, a big raccoon!
We weave dreams into every row,
And sip our tea with a funky glow.

Oh what a riot, our laughter swells,
Creating art, not one, but twelve!
With fuzzy friends and stories spun,
Knitting life, we're never done!

So here we sit, in yarn-filled bliss,
With every stitch, we find our miss.
Embroidered laughter, we can't ignore,
In this woolen world, there's always more!

A Patchwork of Moments

In a world of yarn and cheer,
A tangled mess, yet so sincere.
With needles clacking, laughter spreads,
We stitch our dreams, ignore the threads.

A pattern's lost, but who's to care?
We'll knit a hat, then lose a pair.
From mismatched socks to colorful scarves,
Our creation sings, the joy it carves.

Laughter loops around each stitch,
Grandma's secrets, an endless pitch.
We knot our worries, pull them tight,
With purls of giggles, all feels right.

A patchwork of our silly schemes,
With yarn-filled hearts, we weave our dreams.
Our knitted chaos is pure delight,
In every loop, we find our light.

Gathering Threads of Home

With yarn on couches, scattered wide,
A feline friend seeks to abide.
He pounces on my wooly spree,
I laugh and chase him—how can this be?

In tangled knots, we find our way,
Each slip and stitch gives us sway.
Grandpa's grumbles, Mom's wise cracks,
Each wobbly knit, a love that stacks.

The smell of popcorn fills the room,
As knitting fills our hearts with bloom.
We swap our tales, in thread entwined,
In every fiber, joy we find.

As fingers work, the stories flow,
A family quilt we proudly sew.
Gathering love in every strand,
With quirky stitches, hand in hand.

Resting in Crafted Comfort

With a ball of fluff and cup in hand,
We settle in our cozy land.
Each toss of yarn a gentle tease,
As laughter bubbles, hearts at ease.

In comfy chairs, the patterns fade,
We craft our jokes like homemade braid.
A mismatched sleeve, a lopsided hat,
What's perfection? Let's have a chat!

Bobbling stitches, my mother's pride,
Each silly mistake a joyful ride.
With every purl, a story told,
In crafted comfort, we break the mold.

We dance with yarn, we spin, we thread,
In each soft stitch, our worries shed.
Laughter and love, they intertwine,
In our crafted zone, all things align.

Waves of Woolen Whimsy

With woolen waves, we surf the fun,
A knitted quest, we've just begun.
The colors splash, like ocean tides,
Amidst the chaos, silliness resides.

In tangled loops and playful stares,
We craft our dreams without a care.
Socks that match? That's quite a feat!
We laugh and dance to our own beat.

Crochet hooks become our wands,
As we create in cozy bands.
With cackles echoing through the room,
Even the yarn must feel our zoom!

Whimsy flows in every thread,
A tapestry of laughs we spread.
So grab your yarn, come join the fray,
In waves of wool, we'll laugh away.

Threads of Affection

In the corner sits my yarn,
A tangle that brings me charm.
With needles clicking in a dance,
Each stitch is like a silly prance.

Colorful chaos, a knitted spree,
Who knew crafting could bring such glee?
Pullover mishaps, oh what a sight,
I'll wear my blunders with delight!

Tangled threads on my pet cat's tail,
She struts around like a tiny whale.
I laugh as she trips on my old sock,
In this house, it's a yarn-filled block!

With every loop, a story told,
Of knitwear dreams, both brave and bold.
So grab a skein, let laughter flow,
In this woolly world, joy will grow.

The Serenity of Crafting

Needle in hand, I start my quest,
Unraveling humor, my cozy jest.
My coffee's cold, but who really minds?
I'm crafting smiles that love unwinds.

A scarf for auntie, it's quite the feat,
Looks more like a tangled sheet!
She'll wear it proudly, a badge of art,
Or a funny cape that steals the heart!

My dog thinks my yarn is a toy,
He chews on colors with pure joy.
Each frayed strand tells a cheesy tale,
Of a cozy day where giggles prevail.

With every stitch, the moments stay,
Crafting memories, come what may.
A tapestry of silly in my lap,
Threads of laughter, a warm hug wrap.

Knitted Shadows at Twilight

As twilight falls, my yarn does glow,
In this light, my stitches grow.
With mischief packed in every thread,
I create warmth, not a sweater dread.

Fingers fumble, what a sight,
A stitch gone rogue, taking flight!
My project sits, a lopsided mess,
Each loop a giggle, no need to stress.

The dog snores loud while I create,
In projects lined with family fate.
Haunted by patterns and tangled yarn,
A knitting ghost gives me alarm!

Yet shadows dance as I unwind,
Joy is waiting, oh so kind.
They laugh and twirl, these threads today,
In evening light, we all play.

Touched by Warmth

A yarn ball rolls, it starts a race,
My knitting needles in a chase.
On the couch, oh what a mess,
But warmth is here, and I must confess!

Each color tells a joke or two,
As I knit away, I think of you.
My hat is goofy, my socks askew,
But I wear them bold, like a knitted crew!

My cat naps on a blanket made,
Of every mistake, yet unafraid.
With every stitch, the laughter grows,
In this cozy world, affection flows.

So here we sit in tangled bliss,
Knitting memories that none would miss.
With every loop, the dark fades bright,
Touched by warmth, everything feels right.

Seasons of Softly Knitted Love

Each stitch a hug, so warm and tight,
My cat's mistaken it for a pillow fight.
As yarn unwinds, so do we all,
Fingers dance, and laughter's our call.

In summer, we knit on a sunny patch,
With needles clinking, a merry match.
But winter winds, they sneak right in,
Now scarfs are worn, and chinchillas grin!

Colors clash like socks gone rogue,
Fashion faux pas in a knitted fog.
Yet style's a choice, and I embrace,
Whimsical wear on my happy face!

So come and join the stitch parade,
With tangled yarn, let's serenade.
In every loop and every purl,
We find the joy in this fuzzy whirl.

Memories Stitched in Wool

Grandma's needles click like her witty jokes,
Knit one, purl two, coaxing giggles from folks.
Her yarn basket's a treasure of colors bright,
Where stories unravel on a fiber flight.

Remembering the time I knitted a hat,
It turned to a cozy, oversized mat!
But we wore it proudly, with flair and cheer,
Even the dog gave a snort of sincere.

Once we knitted a blanket for Mom's old chair,
But it also fit the cat, who didn't care!
They curled up together, in cozy delight,
Two furry fools, snoozing through the night.

So here's to the yarn, and all that it brings,
From quirky creations to odd little things.
With every stitch, there's laughter and love,
A soft knitted hug from the heavens above.

Loops of Lazy Afternoon

Laying languidly, with yarn in my lap,
Each twist of the thread is a cozy nap.
On this lazy afternoon, I sip some tea,
As knitting needles dance, just like me.

The ball of yarn rolls right off the chair,
A rabbit escaping, without a care.
I chase it down with a giggle and grin,
But there's a new project that soon will begin!

Birds sing outside, but here's the loot,
Socks that mismatch, oh what a hoot!
Who needs fashion when comfort's the game?
In my knitted chaos, there's never shame.

So let's toast to afternoons wrapped in wool,
Where time drips slow, and hearts are full.
Stitch by stitch, let the fun never end,
In loops and laughter, we'll always blend.

The Embrace of Threaded Tales

In a world of yarn, stories weave and twine,
A silly saga, each stitch, a rhyme.
From socks that could fit a giraffe in a dream,
To scarves long enough to make a stream.

The needles click, in a rhythmic retreat,
As I reminisce of a friend's clumsy feat.
They knitted a sweater that swallowed their head,
A cozy cocoon, thoughts tangled instead!

Each yarn tells tales of laughter and woes,
Of tangled knots and mismatched rows.
But snugly we sit, with warmth in our hearts,
Finding humor in yarn and crafty arts.

So join in the tales that our hands create,
For each fiber spun seals our knit fate.
With laughter in loops and stories unfurled,
Our needlework bonds knit us to the world.

Comfort in Each Loop

With needles clicking, thoughts unwind,
A tangled mess, but joy I find.
Stitches dance in quirky ways,
Laughter blooms on knitting days.

A cat jumps up, a yarnball flies,
My gauge is off, I hear the sighs.
Yet every slip and every drop,
Adds to the charm, I just can't stop.

Colors clash, a riot bright,
A scarf that doubles as a fright.
Grandma's pride, a quirky show,
It's a masterpiece—don't let it go!

In each new scheme, I find my flair,
Endless giggles fill the air.
Yarn tucked snugly, dreams take flight,
Poorly bound, but oh, so right!

Days Spun with Care

With every twist, a tale we share,
As patterns grow, we shed our cares.
Knitting knots and funny slips,
While tangled threads weave friendship's grips.

My partner's scarf, a bright display,
Matches nothing, in a funny way.
The neighbors chuckle, kids all cheer,
It's art—at least, that's what I hear!

Chasing cats and rolling yarn balls,
Projects paused for impromptu brawls.
Knitted chaos, stitches wild,
Life's a circus—and I'm the child.

Soft knots of love, with colors grand,
In laughter, we take a stand.
No perfect finish, just a smile,
In every loop, we love our style!

Yarn-Bound Dreams

In cozy corners, laughs ensue,
As stitches march, a lively crew.
Each purl, each knit, a silly song,
Tangled yarn, where we belong.

A slippery loop, a rogue advance,
My socks dance like they've lost their chance.
"Are those mittens?" friends inquire,
I shrug it off, knitting's my choir.

New yarn purchases spark delight,
"More storage space? Oh what a sight!"
My stash grows thick, a vibrant wall,
A masterpiece? Perhaps, not at all.

With fumbles, stumbles, and bubbly cheer,
We knit our dreams, year after year.
No pattern perfect, just our flair,
In tangled threads, we find repair!

Embracing Threaded Light

With a yarn ball planted on my knee,
I weave the tales of you and me.
As needle dances, giggles flow,
In tangled joy, our spirits grow.

Wobbly stitches, nothing neat,
Each row's a treat, a silly feat.
I knit a hat that's way too wide,
A floppy flop, a joyride.

My friend drops stitches like confetti,
"Try again!" we laugh—so petty!
In yarn-filled shops, decisions blur,
Knit one, purl two—a vibrant stir!

Yet every loop holds laughter tight,
In yarn-bound dreams, we see the light.
So bring your needles, come and stay,
In colorful loops, we'll knit away!

Woven Threads of Solace

On chilly nights with needles whirring,
The clack of yarn starts all the stirring.
A tangled ball, a playful game,
My cat pounces; she thinks it's fame.

Colors clash, a vibrant sight,
I choose purple, then switch to white.
With every stitch, a giggle bursts,
Crafting chaos — oh, how it hurts!

But here I sit, in cozy bliss,
Each loop a hug, a warm caress.
My yarny fortress, snug and tight,
Laughing at life — what pure delight!

Soon I'll wear a mismatched thing,
An oddity that makes me sing.
Though fashion's lost, I've got my cheer,
In woozy threads, there's naught to fear.

Embrace of Yarn and Shadows

In shadows cast by muted light,
I knit away, all feels just right.
A coffee sip, my quiet nook,
The world outside, I simply shook.

My fingers dance among the spools,
As colors merge — who needs the rules?
A scarf for me, a hat for Rob,
A tangled mess? Oh, what a blob!

The yarn unwinds, my patience too,
A knot ties back what I once knew.
I grumble as I start to tease,
Unraveling thoughts; it feels like ease.

Yet when it's done, I'll wear with pride,
A patchwork heart, my crafty guide.
Warmth wrapped around, a cozy glee,
In woven tales, I'm truly free.

Stitches of Serenity

As yarn loops in my morning haze,
I dream of all my crafty ways.
Stitches count as calories, right?
Each purl's a cupcake in my sight!

My cat observes, with eyes so keen,
A ball of fluff, a tiny queen.
My coffee spills, a splash of fate,
Yet still, I knit — oh, isn't it great?

With each new row, I feel the cheer,
A quirky pattern, have no fear.
I drop a stitch, I laugh aloud,
This mishap makes my day quite proud.

A sweater grows from giddy hands,
In knotted realms, we make our plans.
Embrace the fun of every flaw,
In wobbly yarn, we find our awe.

Fiber-Filled Reveries

In evenings soft with flickering light,
I craft a dream that feels just right.
Each yarny twist, a tale unfolds,
In patterns bright, my laughter molds.

My neighbor frowns at my display,
She glances twice, then walks away.
But oh! The joy in every loop,
Who cares? I've made my crazy troop!

The colors fight, they jostle and clash,
A brilliant mess in a happy splash.
With every knit, my heart takes flight,
In this wild world, there's pure delight.

So here's to days wrapped up in fun,
Where laughter grows, and yarn's never done.
With every stitch, my spirit stays,
In fiber-filled, whimsical ways.

Purls of Peace

In a world of tangled threads,
I find my peace in loops and beads.
Yarn may fly and laughter spread,
As cats get tangled, yes indeed!

With needles clicking, stories flow,
Sure, I've stitched a few mishaps.
But with each purl, my worries go,
And coffee spills? Just happy laps!

Each pattern holds a secret mad,
A mix of chaos and delight.
From warmth so cozy, never sad,
To stitches that dance in the night.

So laugh along with this soft art,
For every loop is joy in part.
And if the yarn starts coming apart,
Just grab a cookie, it's a great start!

A Blanket of Gentle Thoughts

Wrapped in yarn, I sit and grin,
Each stitch a thought, a giggly spin.
It's not just warmth that's keeping in,
But fuzzy dreams where laughs begin.

A blanket grows with every snicker,
Odd patterns mark my silly flicker.
The more I knit, the more I bicker,
As yarn balls roll, they just get thicker!

Oh, who knew thoughts could be this warm?
With every loop, a funny charm.
The kittens bat at mittens' form,
While I just laugh, can't take alarm.

So in the folds of woolen delight,
I find my joy, both day and night.
With coffee breaks and yarn in sight,
I stitch my dreams till they're just right!

Knots of Nostalgia

I pull out yarn from days gone by,
Each knot a memory, oh me, oh my!
Who knew that knitting brings a sigh,
With every thread, I reminisce and fly.

A scarf I made in shades of woe,
Turns into laughter, watch them glow!
Each failed stitch points to the show,
Of those wild nights with yarn aglow.

My rusty needles, clumsy hands,
Have captured joy in vibrant strands.
Despite the knots, my heart expands,
Through every memory, life demands.

So here I sit, with yarn to spare,
Creating laughter, everywhere.
My tangled past, a fluffy lair,
Where each knot takes me to old fair!

Stitched Together in Stillness

In quiet moments, I engage,
With yarn so soft, it starts to sage.
Each stitch, a story left on page,
While my cat acts like a sage.

With each new knit, I find a laugh,
A tangled ball, my better half.
As I unravel, oh what a gaffe,
But even chaos makes me chaff!

Woolly wonders fill the air,
Every purl a giggle's stare.
Even when my mind's in despair,
Those little loops bring me to rare.

So here's to days of cozy fun,
Knit and purl until we're done.
In stillness, belly laughs have spun,
While yarn becomes our little sun!

Cozy Reflections in Yarn

In the corner sits my chair,
With my needles, I create,
Stitches fly, oh what a sight,
My cat is plotting yarn's fate.

Purls and knits dance in the air,
Grandma's patterns, a comical mess,
I try to follow, but I swear,
Each blanket's a new type of stress.

Colors clash like a bold cocktail,
Who knew green and purple could fight?
As I stitch, I tell a tale,
Of sweaters that fit like a kite.

In the end, I just love to tease,
These creations may not be gold,
But with laughter and yarn, I seize,
The happiness each loop can hold.

Loops of Laughter

Tangled wool, a messy affair,
Got a tangle? Just scream and shout!
My friends laugh, I don't really care,
Yarn's my buddy, there's no doubt.

Patterns drift from mind to air,
A stitch here, a slip right there,
What's this? A scarf that's round?
I call it the 'fuzzy crown'!

Loop-de-loops and twists galore,
I find a new stitch, fill with glee,
Who knew crafting was like a chore?
Just call me the yarn sorceress, whee!

In my world, it's fun to knit,
Mistakes become a part of art,
With every slip, I must admit,
The joy of yarn just fills my heart!

Tales Wrapped in Wool

Beneath the moon, my yarn spins tales,
Of sweaters that fit like old sails.
Each pattern's a humorous twist,
Like socks that definitely missed!

My needles chatter in the night,
They gossip of stitches, what a sight!
With every loop, a story told,
Of grand designs that never unfold.

Friends pop by, laughing out loud,
At the hat that looks like a cloud.
"Oh dear, what pattern did you choose?"
I shrug, with colorful yarns to use!

Every ball of yarn holds sheer glee,
With every knit, I must simply agree,
These silly tales that we create,
With laughter at our knitting fate!

Stepping into Softness

Slippers made with love and care,
They wobble like ducks, I swear!
Each footstep takes me on a spree,
Of cozy warmth and giggles free.

A cozy blanket on my knee,
Chasing the chill away with glee,
I cuddle deep, a little snug,
Listening to wool's soft, warm hug.

Laughter echoes as I twirl,
In my scarf, I give a whirl.
I may trip, but with delight,
Who knew purls could cause such fright?

So here I sit, with yarn in hand,
Creating joy, it's simply grand!
My many stitches weave a dream,
Of silly slips and laughter's gleam.

Woolen Embraces

In a world of yarn and purls,
I tangled up my thoughts in swirls.
A scarf that never ends in sight,
Keeps me warm on chilly nights.

My cat thinks it's a giant toy,
She pounces and jumps, oh what joy!
With strands of color strewn about,
I trip, I fall, I laugh, I shout.

Each stitch a story, every knit,
A time to pause, a perfect fit.
I often find, with threads entwined,
The giggles caught, in loops confined.

And when my friends come to unwind,
We swap our tales, both sweet and blind.
With needles clicking, hearts align,
We knit together, one design.

Gentle Loops of Memory

In gentle loops, our laughter grows,
With each new stitch, a memory flows.
We knit the past, both soft and bright,
In shades of joy, beyond the night.

My sweater looks quite like a sloth,
Its arms too long, I laugh, I'm caught.
I wear it still, with pride anew,
A badge of honor, a cozy view.

The jumpers sag, the hats bemuse,
Crochet disasters, who can refuse?
Yet as we joke and share our fray,
The warmth we knit won't fade away.

So grab some yarn, let's make a mess,
A comfy space, a woolen dress.
Among the laughs, the tangled cheer,
Memories knit, bound forever near.

The Fabric of Home

In threads of love, we weave our tale,
Where warmth resides, and fears grow pale.
The fabric stretched from floor to door,
It wraps around us, evermore.

A patchwork quilt, so full of pride,
Each square a memory, none can hide.
I spilled my drink, but laughed it off,
This cozy space, our cherished scoff.

When winter bites with icy breath,
We knit and laugh, defy the stress.
The purls of friendship, firmly spun,
Warm hearts unite, we twirl and run.

So long as yarn and joy remain,
Our days are stitched, no thread in vain.
A tapestry of silly glee,
In every loop, you'll find me free.

Tangles of Sweet Rest

In tangled yarns, the laughter blooms,
With every stitch, I greet the goons.
A ball of wool that rolls away,
Becomes my pet on a mad play day.

As needles click, my fingers dance,
With tangled threads, I take a chance.
A snooze or two, amidst my knits,
I wake, my scarf now has some wits!

The cushions stuffed with all my fails,
Are proof of joy, in fuzzy trails.
A tangled mess, but that's okay,
We find our treasures in dismay.

So raise a cup of tea with cheer,
To all our stitches, loud and clear!
For in this craft, we know the best,
Tangles bring us sweet, sweet rest.

Interlaced Silhouettes

In a corner, needles clink,
Yarn dances, colors blink.
Patterns twist, a comic scene,
Socks for cats? Oh, what a dream!

The dog watches, tail a wag,
Caught in wool, a fuzzy snag.
Stitches slip, oh what a mess,
Laughter hides behind the stress.

Cacti wearing knitted hats,
Mice in scarves? Now that's the cat's!
We knit in chaos, what a joy,
Even the yarn joins in the ploy!

As stitches grow and tensions peak,
We find the fun in every leak.
So if you see a tangled thread,
Just laugh it off, then go ahead!

Loopy Days of Contentment

Loops and twists, a tangled dance,
Yarn balls rolling, given chance.
Coffee spills on yarn so bright,
Turning chaos into light.

Needle battles, oh so bold,
Winning stitches, tales retold.
A scarf for grandpa, three feet wide,
He wears it proudly, full of pride.

Is that a hat or battle gear?
Questions asked, no need to fear.
We knit with joy in every row,
Creating warmth, a lively show!

With each purl, we share delight,
Brightened days with every sight.
When the yarn gets knotted tight,
We revel in the silly fight!

Heavy Hearts Lightened by Yarn

The world spins fast, emotions sway,
Grab some yarn, keep worries at bay.
A tangled mess turns into cheer,
With each stitch, we shed a tear.

Grandma's scarf, a legacy rich,
Knitting comforts, fills the niche.
Even socks for mismatched toes,
Bring us laughs, as everyone knows.

How many hats can one head wear?
A competition, do we dare?
Laughter echoes through the room,
As we craft away the gloom.

With every stitch, we mend our hearts,
Unraveling life, stitching parts.
So let the yarn guide your way,
Finding joy in every fray!

Tension Released in Twill

The loom's a friend, a merry beast,
It laughs at tensions, calls for feast.
Yarn on sticks, a wicked fight,
Braid my hair? It looks just right!

Knitting needles spar in jest,
Dueling patterns? Who knits best?
A blanket for a tiny pea,
Or fire-breathing dragon, see?

Yarn bombs on trees, what a sight!
Giggling stitches through the night.
With each loop, we toss the sad,
As laughter swirls, we're never mad.

So here's to yarn, and all it brings,
The joy, the mess, the silly things.
Release the tension, let it slide,
Embrace the laughter, take the ride!

Tangles of Tranquil Time

In a world of yarn and thread,
I tangled dreams while half asleep.
The cat pounced on my lap instead,
Creating chaos every leap.

With needles dancing to a tune,
I crafted hats for all my friends.
One looked like a big balloon,
Muffin tops, oh, where it ends!

The patterns mocked my every try,
Stitches crooked, a wild spree.
Laughter echoed like a sigh,
As I unraveled with glee.

Yet through each slip and every knot,
I found joy in the misfit threads.
For in each mess, a lesson taught,
Life's quirks are what love spreads.

Simple Stitches of Joy

With needles clacking, here we go,
A garland of joy to weave and play.
Each little loop, a smile to show,
Bringing laughter into the fray.

Two left thumbs? Oh, what a sight!
Colors clashing, what a display!
The scarf ended up rather tight,
A fashionable noose, eh, hooray!

In stitches, I found silly tales,
Of grandmas who knit and giggle.
With every slip, the humor prevails,
How yarn can twist and wiggle.

Knitting chaos, a playful art,
With each mistake, a chuckle's made.
Simple stitches, a work of heart,
In laughter we find our serenade.

Soft Stitches of Solitude

In a corner, quiet and bright,
I knit away my daily woes.
With soft yarn balls within my sight,
A cozy world where laughter grows.

Each stitch a giggle, oh so sweet,
As patterns dance and dreams take flight.
A bunny hat that looks quite neat,
Or maybe a sweater fit for fright!

The silence hums a playful tune,
With needles clicking in a spree.
Mistakes? Just a cause to swoon,
Embracing fun, not misery.

In cozy realms, I find my space,
Where solitude wraps me in grace.
And as I weave, a smile takes place,
In soft stitches, life's sweet embrace.

Warmth Woven in Time

In loops that hug like brotherly fun,
Each row a chuckle, a merry dance.
Who knew that yarn could bring such sun?
Laughter twirls in every glance.

With a wild slip and a cheeky grin,
A pattern lost, but oh so bright!
Knitting stories tucked within,
Cozy chaos, pure delight.

Blankets piled high, a fluffy mound,
I tripped and toppled in the heap.
With yarn all tied and tightly bound,
I laughed so hard, I fell asleep.

Time woven gently, stitch by stitch,
Every fiber holds a cheer.
In playful knots, we find our niche,
And warmth that warms each heart so dear.

Quietude in Every Stitch

In a world where loops entwine,
I dropped a stitch, oh what a sign!
My cat claims it with little grace,
Unraveling my peace, just in case.

With needles clicking a goofy tune,
I made a scarf that looks like a moon.
I wore it proudly on a bright sunny day,
Feeling like a fashion model, come what may.

I knitted socks that don't quite fit,
One for each foot, they sure do split.
My friends just laugh, they think it's a game,
But trust me, my feet are never the same!

So here I sit, amidst yarn and cheer,
Crafting odd hats that draw in the peer.
Each odd creation brings smiles my way,
And that, my friend, is my perfect day.

Handheld Joys in Yarn

With every purl and every knit,
I craft a scarf that's rather fit.
It's more like a snake, quite long and thin,
My dog loves it, he thinks it's a win!

The ball of yarn rolls away in haste,
Chasing it feels like a silly race.
Neighbors gaze out as I twirl and dive,
They wonder if I'm truly alive!

Oh, look at this hat, so wonderfully round,
It looks like a mushroom, it's quite profound.
I wear it out while sipping my tea,
Strangers just smile, what could this be?

Each tangled thread's a story untold,
Of mishaps and laughter, of warmth in the cold.
Yarn in my hands, I'm the queen of the fun,
In a world of stitches, I've already won!

The Serenity of Handcrafted Times

In a crafty nook with tea and lace,
I grapple my yarn in a crazy chase.
My knitting needles dance and clash,
Creating mishaps, oh what a splash!

With yarn explosions and tangled threads,
My cat joins in on this crazy spread.
She pounces and rolls, a furry delight,
Making my efforts a comical sight.

In my hand, a project begins to unwind,
A bumpy blanket, oh what a find!
My friends laugh hard, they can't get enough,
This mess, my dear, is just perfect fluff!

So here's to my craft, with humor and cheer,
Each stitch a giggle, each loop a dear.
For laughter and yarn, I'll forever pursue,
In this cozy chaos, it's just me and you.

Colors of Comfort

With every hue, I play and swatch,
A rainbow scarf—the colors they botch!
A red and green mix like Christmas gone wild,
A confused little fashionista, so beguiled.

The skeins of yarn dance in rows,
While I sit here perplexed, nobody knows.
"This sweater looks great!" I cry with glee,
But it's three sizes too big for me!

I tried to knit a lovely pair of mitts,
But ended up with pancake bits.
My hands are cold but my heart is warm,
In this zany craft, I find my charm!

Colors collide like a circus parade,
In this yarn universe, I've surely strayed.
Yet, amidst the giggles and playful fray,
I find joy in colors, come what may!

Knitting a Universe of Dreams

In the yarn of my thoughts, I weave,
A galaxy spun with every sleeve.
Socks for planets that never pair,
And mittens that float in cosmic air.

Upside-down sweaters, a fashion faux pas,
I'm crafting a life that's full of 'aha!'
With needles like wands, I conjure delight,
In a blanket of laughter, I snuggle up tight.

Balls of wool roll like runaway cars,
Arguing with gravity, avoiding the stars.
Each tangled mess tells a tale of its own,
While I sip my tea and scribble on my phone.

So here's to the stitches, to laughter and yarn,
To the quirky creations that make my heart warm.
In my knitted cosmos, we dance and we play,
Building a universe in a colorful way.

Each Stitch a Story

With every stitch, a giggle escapes,
Purling together our wild mishaps.
Yarn balls chase each other around,
Knots in my head, like lost socks, are found.

A scarf that's bumpy, a hat that's too tight,
Fashion disasters create quite the sight.
My pet cat, a model, wears knitted pride,
In sweaters so bright, she cannot decide.

I am a wizard, with loops and a twist,
Creating odd things that simply can't exist.
Every yarn drama makes my heart swell,
As I laugh with my stitches, oh, can't you tell?

So let's knit a tale, full of zest and cheer,
Of sweaters that sing and hats that may sneer.
In the tapestry of joy, we find our delight,
Each stitch a giggle, a whimsical flight.

Breath Among the Fiber

In a land where yarn and laughter collide,
I breathe in colors, let chaos be my guide.
Socks with stripes that never match,
A statement of silliness, oh, what a catch!

With needles clicking like tiny drum beats,
I create a symphony from mismatched fleets.
A blanket of quirky, a vest for my cat,
Each project a puzzle that leads to a spat.

Yarns whisper softly with tales to unfold,
Of frizzy-haired puppets that once were bold.
In this world of fiber, the fun never ends,
As I cozy up tight with my woolly friends.

So let's take a breath in the softest embrace,
And dance through the days in this fuzzy space.
With laughter entwined in each fluffy thread,
We'll knit our adventures, where joys are spread.

Whispers of Warm Fabric

Amidst the yarn, sweet whispers arise,
Secret stories spun under the skies.
Each thread a giggle, a chuckle, a cheer,
As I wrap myself in warmth, oh dear!

Knit one, purl two, what could go wrong?
A hat that resembles a pumpkin, so strong!
With patterns resembling a confused maze,
I weave my own chaos in glorious ways.

Cuddly blankets love to gossip and tease,
About all of my projects that don't quite please.
Yet each silly stitch is a tale from my heart,
In the world of warm fabric, I play my part.

So let's hear the whispers of laughter and cheer,
As I embrace yarn with joy, never fear.
In the threads of our lives, let's knit something bright,
In the comfort of moments that spark pure delight.

Embracing the Cozy Hours

In a chair with yarn galore,
I start to dream and snore.
A cat leaps high, lands with a twist,
And all my stitches go to mist.

The needles click, a tap dance tune,
My sweater grows like a balloon.
With every loop, I chance a grin,
And wonder where my days begin.

Coffee spills on my latest feat,
Garnet stains on cozy seat.
Each misstep, a tale to spin,
In this house where quirks begin.

My friend drops by with a frown and tea,
"Did you even knit? Or just sip for spree?"
I hold my work with a proud laugh,
"Artistic license, you do the math!"

Patterns in the Soft Light

Patterns dance on the wall,
As yarn welcomes every fall.
With a tangle here, and a knot right there,
I'm creating masterpieces, I swear!

A strange loop hides in the weave,
Giving pause for jokes conceived.
"Did you plan that?" they ask in jest,
I chuckle, "Of course—it's my best!"

As daylight fades, my ideas sprout,
Each stitch a vision, no doubt,
But then a slip, and oh dear me!
I'm knitting spaghetti, not a tee!

With friends around, laughter bursts,
In tangled tales, we quench our thirst.
For every drop, and every dream,
This soft light casts a cozy scheme.

Comfort in Every Loop

With loops and whorls, I take my stand,
My knitting needles, a magical wand.
A scarf that's longer than my pet,
"Do we need to measure? Not just yet!"

Frogged my work, it jumped away,
"Not a froggy here, just a yarn ballet!"
Each mistake, a giggle anew,
As stitches race, and chaos grew.

The clock ticks on, but I'm ensnared,
In a sea of yarn, I'm unprepared.
Chasing loops like a silly hare,
My friends remind me, "There's knitting to share!"

In every twist, there's joy to find,
A world that's warm, where hearts unwind.
So let's embrace this playful spree,
Where every loop becomes a decree.

Frayed Edges of Reflection

Frayed edges tell stories untold,
Of missed stitches in knits so bold.
Each snag a laugh, a lesson learned,
In the tangle of life, my heart has turned.

Through mischief and yarn, I weave a plot,
Where laughter flows and worries are not.
A little tug and a playful dance,
In this crafting world, I take my chance.

The mirror mocks, with yarn in my hair,
"Did you knit or just lose a dare?"
With a wink and a sip of my brew,
I simply reply, "Just part of the crew!"

So here I am, with threads so wild,
In knotted charm, I'm nature's child.
With friends and yarn, the fun thrives great,
In every frayed edge, life's quirky fate.

Comfort Found in Every Loop

In a world of loops and twists,
Where every stitch is full of bliss,
I stumble through a yarny haze,
A weaving wizard in a daze.

The cat now claims my yarny prize,
With tangled threads, he plays and flies,
While needles dance, I sip my tea,
A circus act, oh look at me!

Each row I knit, a story told,
Of close-knit friends and hearts of gold,
With every purl, a giggle flows,
As on my lap, the cat now doze.

So here I sit, my castle grand,
With tangled yarn in clumsy hand,
With every loop, I find my fun,
In knotted days, I'm never done.

Days Spun in Soft Yarn

In a pile of colors, I get lost,
A skein of laughter — what a cost!
With every twist, a wiggly cheer,
As needles click, my worries disappear.

I frolic in fibers, oh what a sight,
My dog steals yarn — what a funny fright!
He prances proud, my woolly thief,
As I chase him, a scene of relief.

Grandma chuckles from way down the lane,
With her secret stash tucked right where it's plain,
"If you think this is funny," she says with a grin,
"Wait till you see the mess that you've spun!"

So here we weave, with giggles and spun,
Creating a tapestry, laughter won,
In every stitch, a joke or a pun,
These days of yarn, oh how they run!

Texture of Everyday Magic

In the art of knitting, strange spells arise,
With yarn in hand, I conjure surprise,
A mystical craft of sticks and thread,
Where laughter's the yarn, and joy's widely spread.

I tripped on my needles, what a clatter!
The cat now sits, as if in a patter,
While I fall sideways, it's all gone wrong,
Yet somehow still, I hum a silly song.

Each project brings trials I never forsee,
A scarf turned into a hat — oh dear me!
The patterns unwieldy, yet laughs are found,
In every blunder, good times abound.

So here's to the moments of tangled delight,
With yarn softly whispering through the night,
In stitches and giggles, the magic will flow,
As we knit our stories from scratch, to and fro.

A Tangle of Cozy Memories

A ball of yarn rolls under the chair,
I chase after giggles, it's quite the affair,
With each little tug, a memory's spun,
Of sunny days shared, oh what fun!

In grandmas' quilts, a whole world resides,
With laughter and whispers, where warmth collides,
The cat finds solace, lords over his throne,
While I stitch together these moments we've known.

Each knot tells a tale of joyful embrace,
As needles join in a soft, rhythmic race,
And though I may stumble, in stitches I keep,
The laughter we share, in my heart it will leap.

So here's to the tangles that life seems to bring,
In a whirlwind of yarn, my spirit will sing,
With every loop, a loving decree,
In cozy creations, we find unity.

Twists and Turns of Tranquility

In a ball of yarn, I find my glee,
Purling my worries, sipping my tea.
Mocking the cat when she tries to play,
Chasing loose strands that lead her astray.

Loops and knots dance with grace so bold,
Each stitch a secret, a story told.
I laugh at the chaos, the tangled spree,
A masterpiece waiting, just let it be.

My needles click rhythm, a gentle tune,
Like whispers of cozy from morning to noon.
The world outside fades, who needs the sun?
With woolen armies, my battles are won.

So here in my den, I take the chance,
To spin out my yarn in a quirky dance.
With each little twist, life becomes clear,
In my crafty haven, I shed every fear.

Cozy Whispers in Wool

Woolly whispers wrapped snug and tight,
Every stitch echoes soft delight.
The dog sneaks a nibble, oh, what a bite,
He thinks he's a goat in the dead of night.

A rainbow of colors sprawls on my floor,
Like a candy shop mixed with folklore.
I giggle as I trip on my own creation,
Knitting my dreams without hesitation.

My grandma's old patterns a treasure, indeed,
I follow her legacy, stitch by stitch, heed.
Feather-light laughter floats through the air,
While rogue balls of yarn roll everywhere.

With a cup of hot cocoa, I sit, just so,
Knitting my worries, letting them go.
Life tangled in stitches, oh, what a sight,
In this warm wooly world, everything's right.

Threads of Time and Tenderness

With each little loop, I weave my thoughts,
Creating a blanket of joyful spots.
The clock's ticking slowly, like yarn in a spin,
While my needles click on, let the mischief begin.

A stitch here for laughter, a knot there for love,
My yarn starts to hum, like a sock from above.
Stitches speak softly, a humorous plea,
To keep all my worries as far as can be.

Puppies and yarn will engage in a fight,
While I trace the edges of dark and light.
Fingers all tangled, a dance so sweet,
My floor's the new runway for crafty feet.

Laughter erupts at the twisted designs,
As I wrestle with yarn in peculiar lines.
In a world wrapped in fabric, I find my way,
With threads of time and a splash of play.

Knots of Peaceful Moments

In the corner I stitch, with humor and cheer,
While the music of needles fills up the sphere.
The children unite, they tangle my thread,
But laughter erupts, and joy is widespread.

I try knitting socks, but they turn into hats,
The cat makes the rounds, oh, she's such a brat!
With each little twist, my worries grow light,
In knots of distraction, my day turns out bright.

The couch becomes home to yarn monsters galore,
While friends drop by with gossip and more.
We giggle and sip tea, in this crafty zone,
Creating a mess, but we're never alone.

In the whirl of the wool and the chatter we weave,
Each moment we share is one to believe.
So here I will stay, in love and in laughter,
With knotted up memories and joy ever after.

Embracing the Slow Pace

In a world that whirls with haste,
I find joy in every paste.
Stitch by stitch, my worries fade,
In cozy yarns, I'm blissfully laid.

My needles dance like disco balls,
With tangled threads and playful falls.
A loop, a twist, a joyful nick,
Life is better with a click and tick.

I sip my tea while stitches grow,
A haven found in every row.
The clock can tick, but I'll just stay,
In my yarny castle, come what may.

So let the frantic rush go by,
I'll stay put and knit, oh my!
For in this world of laughter and threads,
I find my peace where joy spreads.

Tranquil Threads

With woolly wonders in my lap,
I take my time, it's quite the map.
Softest fibers in my hand,
Creating chaos, unplanned.

I drop a stitch, oh what a sight!
My pet cat thinks it's pure delight.
She pounces in, a fuzzy blur,
While I just laugh, oh that little fur.

The yarn's entangled in a mess,
A maze of colors, I confess.
But in this chaos, giggles bloom,
As patterns knit in yarny room.

With every snip and playful poke,
I weave my dreams in every joke.
Tranquil threads that make me smile,
Let's knit our worries for a while.

Memories of Happy Stitches

Each yarn holds stories, knit with cheer,
In cozy corners, love draws near.
A slipped stitch brings forth a grin,
A funky hat? Oh, let's begin!

The moment when my scarf went long,
I wore it proudly, felt so strong.
Yet in the wind, it flew away,
Who needs a scarf on a bright day?

A ball of yarn rolled past the door,
A chase ensued, I laughed some more.
My family joins this woolly game,
In stitches and purls, we wind our name.

From family tales to crafted glee,
Each stitch brings memories to me.
With laughter woven in our seams,
We stitch together all our dreams.

Knitted Bliss of Everyday

In the realm of yarn and wool,
Life becomes a gentle pull.
Knit one, purl two, oh what fun,
With every row, I'm brightly spun.

My coffee spills, the yarn unwinds,
But laughter's where true joy finds.
With every oops, a new design,
A ballet of colors, oh mine, oh mine!

The neighbor's dog thinks I'm a tree,
He jumps right in, and oh, just see!
My needles fly in frantic chase,
As we both share this happy space.

In knitted bliss, the day drifts by,
A tapestry of laughter, oh my!
So here I sit with yarn in hand,
In a world where joy is always planned.

Milton Keynes UK
Ingram Content Group UK Ltd.
UKHW030750121124
451094UK0C013B/820